SINGIN'

with the

SAINTS

DYNAMIC PRAISE *for* MEN

ARRANGED *by*

RUSSELL MAULDIN

Lillenas PUBLISHING COMPANY

KANSAS CITY, MO 64141

Contents

Psalms of Praise

Words and Music by
ANTHONY WILKINS
and **PATRICK HENDERSON**
Arranged by Tom Fettke
TTBB arr. by Russell Mauldin

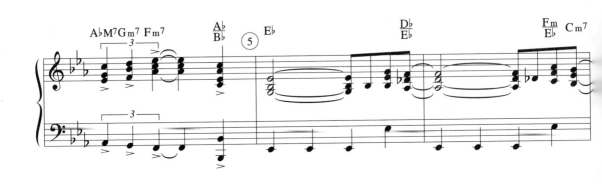

© 1990 Birdwing Music/Patrick Fleming Music (ASCAP).
All rights administered by EMI Christian Music Publishing. Used by permission.

PLEASE NOTE: Copying of this product is not covered by CCLI licenses. For CCLI information call 1-800-234-2446.

Lord, all ye peo - ple of the Lord, Stand and

praise _____ Him in the house of ___ the

Lord. Praise ye the Lord, all ye

8

12

Holy, You Are Holy

Words and Music by
BRUCE WICKERSHEIM
Arranged by Richard Kingsmore
TTBB arr. by Russell Mauldin

CD: 11

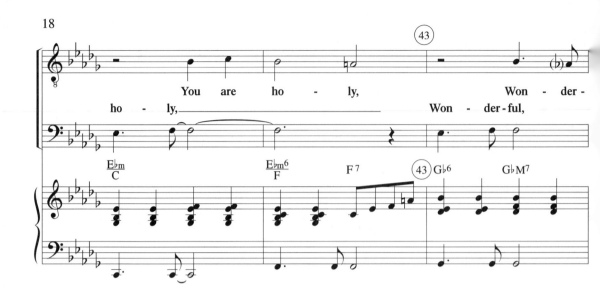

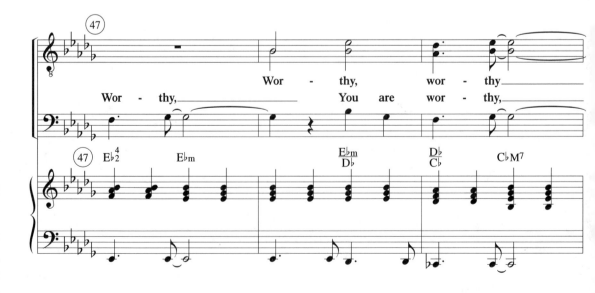

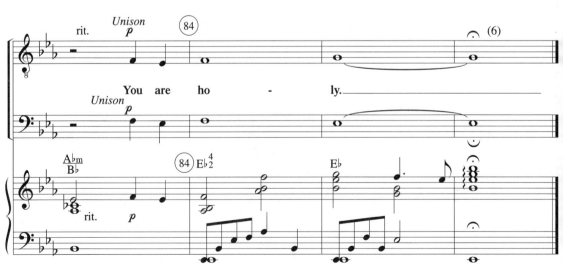

Singing with the Saints

Words and Music by
JOHN ROWSEY, JOHN STARNES
and DARYAL WILLIAMS
Arranged by Russell Mauldin

CD: 15

-ty's gon - na start and go   on   and   on_____ and   on.____

And I'll be   sing - in' with the saints   at the

morn - in'   light,_____ Ring - in' in the day   'cause there

Well, the tam-bou-rine's ring-in' and Da - vid starts to feel the rhy -

- thm._____ Paul and Si - las are hum - min' a tune__

_____ they wrote in pris - on._____ Well, Ga-

CD: 17

- briel hears the mu - sic and he picks up his horn;_____ It's just____ an - oth - er glo - ry, hal - le - lu - jah morn!_____ And I'll be sing - in' with the saints at the

morn - in' light,_____ Ring - in' in the day 'cause there

is no night;_____ Say - in' good - bye to the

heart-ache, trou-ble and pain._____ I'll be sit -

More

Words and Music by
SCOTT KRIPPAYNE, TONY MIRACLE
and CHARLIE PEACOCK
Arranged by Dennis Allen
TTBB arr. by Russell Mauldin

CD: 23

(to pg. 38, meas. 5)

(to pg. 38, meas. 5)

more.

CD: 25

You are my Sav - ior, my Re - deem - er and my Friend. _____ You

44

In the Presence of Jehovah

Words and Music by
GERON DAVIS
Arranged by Marty Parks
TTBB arr. by Russell Mauldin

All day long I strug - gle_____ for an - swers that I need. Then I come in - to His pres - ence, and all my ques - tions be - come clear. And for a sa - cred

48

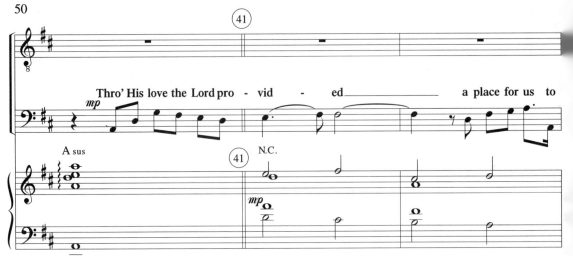

Thro' His love the Lord pro - vid - ed___ a place for us to

rest;___
A place to find the an - swer___

___ in hours___ of dis - tress.
There is nev-er an - y

Jesus Christ Is the Lord of All

Words and Music by
DAN WHITTEMORE
Arranged by Camp Kirkland and Tom Fettke
TTBB arr. by Russell Mauldin

pres - i - dents, princ - es, rul - ers and Kings,

who of all____ shall reign su - preme?

57

heav - en's pow-ers and au-thor - i - ties,___
once His en - e - my___ in___ our minds,___

on - ly He___ is De - i - ty.___
by His blood___ His peace we find.___

Je - sus,___ Je - sus, Je-sus Christ___ is the Lord of all.

62

Jesus Lifted Me

He Lifted Me
I'm So Glad Jesus Lifted Me

Arranged by Camp Kirkland
TTBB arr. by Russell Mauldin

PLEASE NOTE: Copying of this product is not covered by CCLI licenses. For CCLI information call 1-800-234-2446.

*"I'm So Glad Jesus Lifted Me"

70

Je - sus lift - ed me._____

$\frac{G}{D}$　　D7　　G

94 half-time feel　　*Optional solo*

I'm____ so glad_____ O__

I'm　　so　　glad_____ Je - sus lift - ed me.__

94 Ab7　　　　　　　　　　Eb　　　$\frac{Fm}{Eb}$ Eb

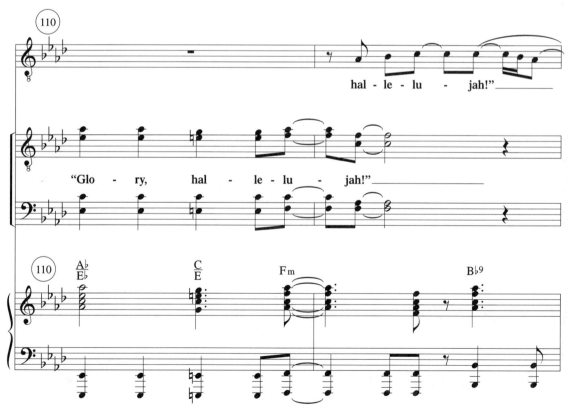

Je - sus lift - ed me.

115 molto rit.

He lift-ed me!

He lift - ed me!

molto rit.

Shine on Us

Words and Music by
MICHAEL W. SMITH
and DEBORAH SMITH
Arranged by Bruce Greer
TTBB arr. by Russell Mauldin

1. Lord, let Your light, light__ of Your
2. Lord, let Your grace, grace__ from Your

80

CD: 46

(to pg. 78, meas. 7)

Let Your light shine on us.

Let Your grace fall on

CD: 48

life,_____ To find our way_____ in the dark - est

night._____ *Unison sub. mf* Let Your

Unison sub. mf

love come_ o - ver us. Let Your

sub. mf

Testify to Love

Words and Music by
**PAUL FIELD, HENK POOL,
RALPH VAN MANEN and ROBERT RIEKIRK**
Arranged by Dennis Allen
TTBB arr. by Russell Mauldin

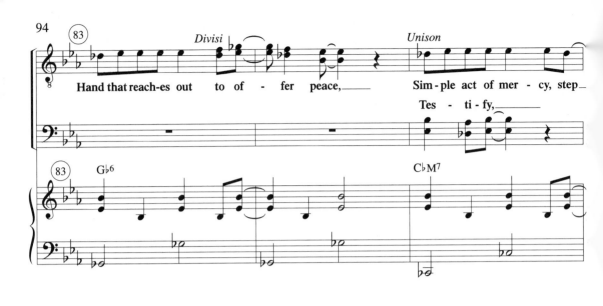

Hand that reach-es out to of - fer peace,___ Sim - ple act of mer - cy, step___

Tes - ti - fy,___

___ to king-dom come, Ev - ery heart will speak what love___ has done.___

tes - ti - fy.___

I will tes - ti - fy.___ For as long___

Call Home

Words and Music by
MOSIE LISTER
Arranged by Mosie Lister
TTBB arr. by Russell Mauldin

There is a mo - ment that lives for - ev - er;
In God's own mem - 'ry it nev - er dies.

Unison 25
Call the Fa - ther; call home.

Unison

D 25 A⁶ A⁷ A⁹ D

3 29
Divisi
Do you re - mem - ber how much He

Divisi
3

D G/A A A
3 29

Unison 33 **CD: 60**
loves you? Wait no long - er; Call

Unison

G/D D D⁶ 33 A⁶ A⁷

All Ye People

Words and Music by
CHRISTOPHER MACHEN
Arranged by Richard Kingsmore
TTBB arr. by Russell Mauldin

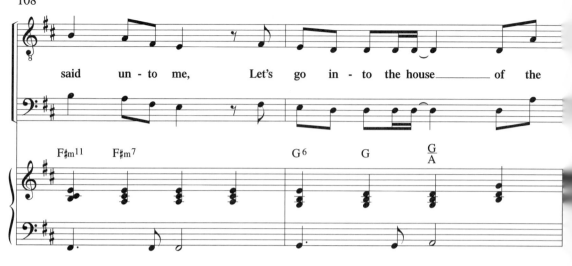

said un - to me, Let's go in - to the house_____ of the

Lord. Cel - e - brate, Let us

sing and re - joice, In one re - sound - ing voice, In

one re - sound - ing voice.

Praise the Lord! All ye peo - ple, All ye

peo - ple, Praise the Lord!

Give Him hon - or, give Him glo - ry, Praise ye the Lord.

Eb(no 3)   Ab   Bb   Eb   N.C.

Ev-er-y-bod - y shout and sing, Praise ye the Lord,

F(no 3)   Bb   C   F

CD: 70

Je-sus is___ the King of Kings.___ Praise ye,___ praise ye___ the

F(no 3)   Bb   C   Am7   BbM7   Am7

Hard Trials Will Soon Be Over

Words and Music t
MOSIE LISTE
Arranged by Marty Par
TTBB arr. by Russell Mauldi

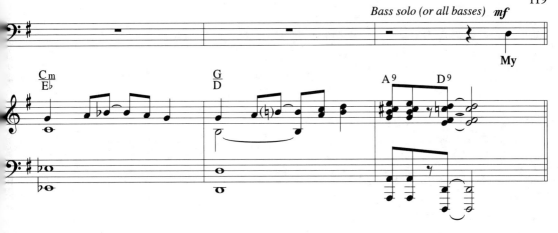

Bass solo (or all basses) *mf*

My

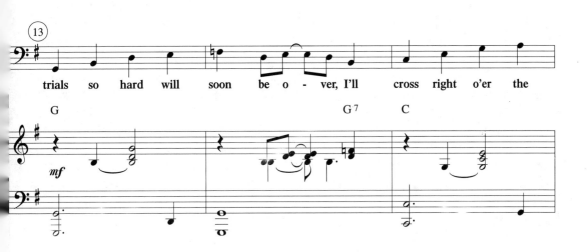

trials so hard will soon be o - ver, I'll cross right o'er the

chil - ly Jor - dan, And there some - where in Heav - en's cit - y I'll

120

*Bass solo continues until meas. 24